Masters of Music
THE WORLD'S GREATEST COMPOSERS

The Life and Times of

Leonard Bernstein

Mitchell Lane
PUBLISHERS

P.O. Box 196
Hockessin, Delaware 19707

Masters of Music
THE WORLD'S GREATEST COMPOSERS

Titles in the Series

The Life and Times of...

Johann Sebastian Bach
Ludwig van Beethoven
Irving Berlin
Hector Berlioz
Leonard Bernstein
Johannes Brahms
Frederic Chopin
Duke Ellington
Stephen Foster
George Gershwin
William Gilbert and Arthur Sullivan
George Frideric Handel
Franz Joseph Haydn
Scott Joplin
Franz Liszt
Felix Mendelssohn
Wolfgang Amadeus Mozart
Franz Peter Schubert
John Philip Sousa
Igor Stravinsky
Peter Ilyich Tchaikovsky
Giuseppe Verdi
Antonio Lucio Vivaldi
Richard Wagner

Visit us on the web: www.mitchelllane.com
Comments? email us: mitchelllane@mitchelllane.com

Masters of Music

THE WORLD'S GREATEST COMPOSERS

The Life and Times of

Leonard Bernstein

by Jim Whiting

Printing   1   2   3   4   5   6   7   8
        Library of Congress Cataloging-in-Publication Data
Whiting, Jim, 1943-
        The life and times of Leonard Bernstein/Jim Whiting.
                p. cm. — (Masters of music)
        Includes bibliographical references (p.) and index.
                ISBN 1-58415-275-3 (library bound)
        1. Leonard Bernstein, 1918—Juvenile literature. 2. Musicians—United States—Biography—Juvenile literature. I. Title. II. Masters of music
(Mitchell Lane Publishers)
ML3930.B48W55 2004
780'.92—dc22

                                                        2004009314

ABOUT THE AUTHOR: Jim Whiting has been a journalist, writer, editor, and photographer for more than 20 years. In addition to a lengthy stint as publisher of *Northwest Runner* magazine, Mr. Whiting has contributed articles to the *Seattle Times*, *Conde Nast Traveler*, *Newsday*, and *Saturday Evening Post*. He has written and edited more than 100 Mitchell Lane titles. His love of music led him to write this book. He lives in Washington state with his wife and two teenage sons.

PUBLISHER'S NOTE: This story is based on the author's extensive research, which he believes to be accurate. Documentation of such research is contained on page 47.

The internet sites referenced herein were active as of the publication date. Due to the fleeting nature of some web sites, we cannot guarantee they will all be active when you are reading this book.

Contents

The Life and Times of
Leonard Bernstein

by Jim Whiting

* For Your Information

German citizens climb through a hole punched in the Berlin Wall shortly after the collapse of the communist regime in East Germany in 1990. Erected nearly 30 years earlier, the wall separated East Berlin from West Berlin and was a symbol of the oppressive East German government.

The Wall Comes Tumbling Down

It was about mid-afternoon on August 17, 1962. A pair of 18-year-old Germans, Peter Fechter and Helmut Kulbeik, hid in the momentary shelter of a deserted lumberyard in communist-controlled East Berlin. They looked across a vacant lot at a six-foot-high concrete wall that was topped with a layer of barbed wire. On the other side lay West Berlin and freedom. The two young men wanted to escape their harsh living conditions under communist rule. Peter had another reason for wanting to cross the wall into West Berlin. His sister lived there. He hadn't seen her for nearly a year.

The two young men each drew a deep breath. Then they took off sprinting as fast as their legs could carry them. Within moments they arrived at the base of the wall. Helmut quickly hoisted himself to the top, hurtled over the barbed wire, and dropped to the other side. He was safe.

Peter was only a few steps behind. He reached the wall and began to scramble upward. Several guards raised their automatic weapons and fired at Peter. Bullets ripped into his back. He fell and lay crumpled at the base of the wall. But he wasn't dead.

Writhing in pain, he screamed, *"Hilfe! Hilfe!"* ("Help! Help!"). The guards ignored his cries.

Hundreds of horrified people on the other side of the wall witnessed the grim scene. They too heard Peter's anguished cries, but there was nothing they could do except scream at the guards. The onlookers included a few American soldiers. One of them called his superior officer. He wanted to do something to help Peter, even if it meant getting into a firefight with the guards on the other side of the wall. The superior officer's response was crystal clear: "Lieutenant, you have your orders. Stand fast. Do nothing."[1]

Over the next hour, Peter's cries gradually diminished. Finally they stopped. Peter Fechter had bled to death. The guards who had watched him die walked over to the lifeless body. They scooped up the teenager's corpse and carried it away.

Peter was one of scores of people who were killed at the Berlin Wall as they tried to escape their country. The wall had a tragic history that dated back to 1945 with the defeat of Germany in World War II. Germany was divided among the four major Allies, the victors in the conflict—the United States, Great Britain, France, and the Soviet Union.

As soon as the war was over, tensions among the Allies emerged. The Soviet Union had a communist government that was vastly different from the other three occupying powers. The Soviets soon pulled away, and their sector became known as East Germany. The rest of Germany was called West Germany. Berlin, the capital, lay deep inside East Germany, and it was also divided into east and west sectors. As the years went by, West Germany became much more prosperous than East Germany. Many East Germans wanted to cross into West Germany to take advantage of the higher standard of living. The border was heavily patrolled.

It was difficult for East Germans to escape. On the other hand, it was relatively easy for them to cross over into West Berlin. Soviet and East German authorities became alarmed at the number of people who were leaving.

On the morning of August 13, 1961, the authorities sealed the border between the two parts of the city and began building what became known as the Berlin Wall. There were only a few openings in the wall, and they were heavily guarded. The most famous of these was Checkpoint Charlie, where U.S. Army soldiers faced East German troops only a few yards away. In addition to the wall itself, they cleared a "death strip," a sandy stretch 100 yards wide that ran along the base of the wall.

Despite the death of Peter and others, people kept trying to get through the Berlin Wall. Most were killed or captured. The Berlin Wall remained a sign of dictatorship and oppression for decades.

With the fall of the Soviet Union and the East German government late in 1989, the wall was finally opened. The Germans celebrated. Much of their pent-up emotion was released during a pair of Christmas concerts that year. One took place in East Berlin and the other in West Berlin. Symbolically, the orchestra included members from both West and East Germany. Other musicians came from the Soviet Union, France, Great Britain, and the United States. There was no question about the music that would be played. It would be the Ninth Symphony, a monumental work by German composer Ludwig van Beethoven. The final movement includes a poem entitled "Ode to Joy," by another German, Friedrich Schiller, which Beethoven set to music. Soloists and chorus sing one of the most famous melodies in music history. It has been used in movies such as *Die Hard, Changing Lanes,* and *Ace Ventura: Pet Detective,* television shows such as *Buffy the Vampire Slayer,* countless advertisements, and even a cellular phone ring.

Somewhat surprisingly, the conductor of the two concerts wasn't a German. He was an American named Leonard Bernstein. His selection was appropriate. For much of his life, Bernstein had stood for freedom—artistically and socially.

Bernstein made one change in Schiller's words. He replaced the word *Freude* (joy) with *Freiheit* (freedom). That way Beethoven's masterpiece would reflect the joy that Germans felt as they regained their freedom.

The change proved to be very effective. As one member of the orchestra recalled, "When the chorus sang the word 'Freiheit' . . . I shall always remember how his [Bernstein's] face lit up."[2]

It may have been the culminating moment of one of the most extraordinary careers in music history. As a conductor, composer, pianist, and teacher, Leonard Bernstein was responsible for lighting up countless numbers of faces.

ON THE BRINK OF NUCLEAR WAR

President Kennedy

Not long after the construction of the Berlin Wall, President John F. Kennedy had a far greater crisis on his hands. On October 16, 1962, he called a meeting of his closest advisers. A routine overflight of Cuba by the U.S. Central Intelligence Agency (CIA) the previous day had revealed that Soviet nuclear missiles were in the process of being installed there. Cuba was less than 100 miles from the coast of Florida. Nearly half of the United States would be within range of these deadly missiles.

Kennedy knew he had to respond. Three options emerged. One was to try to resolve the problem through diplomacy. No one believed that this would do much good. A second was a direct invasion of Cuba, but this could quickly involve the Soviet Union and their massive arsenal of nuclear weapons. A third was a naval blockade of Cuba to prevent further missile shipments from arriving and force the removal of the ones already in place. This plan was risky. The Soviets could choose to defend their ships with their large submarine fleet. They could also put pressure on American forces in other parts of the world.

After five days of intense discussions conducted in complete secrecy, Kennedy decided on the blockade. Then he went on national television to inform the American people about the threat. For nearly a week, the world appeared to be on the brink of war. The Soviets refused to back down. Their ships drew closer and closer to the waiting U.S. naval forces. A U.S. plane was shot down and its pilot was killed. The CIA reported that five missile sites were fully operational. U.S. armed forces were placed on their highest-ever level of readiness.

Then, when it appeared that a nuclear holocaust was inevitable, Soviet Premier Nikita Khrushchev agreed to a deal. His ships would not challenge the blockade. He would remove the missiles from Cuba. In return, the United States would agree not to invade Cuba. American missiles in Turkey would be dismantled.

With this agreement, the Cuban Missile Crisis was over. In 2000, the highly praised film *Thirteen Days* dramatized the events of the Cuban Missile Crisis.

This photo of Leonard Bernstein with his parents Jennie and Samuel was taken in 1921, when Leonard was about three. At this time Leonard was the couple's only child, though Jennie and Samuel would eventually have two more children. At first, Leonard's father opposed his son's musical ambitions, but eventually realized how gifted his son was.

The Discovery of Music

Leonard Bernstein was born on August 25, 1918, in Lawrence, Massachusetts, a town about 20 miles north of Boston. His parents were Samuel and Jennie Bernstein. Both of them had immigrated to the United States from Russia in the early 20th century.

During his boyhood in Russia, Samuel became well educated. Several of his relatives were rabbis, and Samuel studied Jewish texts such as the Torah and Talmud. Yet his family was poor. At that time, there was a great deal of anti-Semitism, or prejudice against Jews, in Russia. Many Jews were injured or killed in unprovoked attacks. Just as bad, it was common for Jews to be drafted into the army as teenagers and compelled to serve for upward of 20 years. Samuel's uncle Harry had escaped from these dismal prospects and gone to the United States. He began working in a barbershop and sent his nephew some money. Without telling his parents, Samuel set out to follow his uncle. After a difficult journey, he arrived in the United States. His first job was cleaning and gutting fish. He often worked 12-hour days, six days a week. Several years later he was fortunate to get a job with Harry, who had opened his own barbershop. Harry hired Samuel to keep the shop clean. In spite of all his hardships, Samuel remained optimistic. He believed that if he worked hard enough, he could improve his life.

Jennie had come to the United States with her family. Like many immigrants, they had trouble making ends meet. When Jennie was 12, she had to go to work in a nearby woolen mill. It was boring work with long hours, and she hated it.

Jennie met Samuel in 1916. By then, he had a good job as assistant manager with a company that sold wigs, cosmetics, and supplies to barbershops. Even though she wasn't especially attracted to him, they were married about a year later.

"It was an unhappy arrangement from the start," according to author Paul Myers. "Sam retained his love of traditional Hebrew studies, and his life was dictated by his religion, his business ambitions and his determination to achieve social acceptance and status. Jennie, who had left school to work at the mill, was not an intellectual. Where Sam was serious, she was pretty, charming, frivolous and intelligently bright but lacking true education. While Sam's head remained buried in the Torah {the book of Jewish law}, she read romantic novels and popular magazines, and it is more than likely that she married him because he provided an escape from life at the mill."[1]

The young couple rented an apartment in Boston. They quickly realized how little they had in common. It didn't help that Samuel looked down on Jennie's parents. Jennie left Samuel for a brief time just before Leonard was born. She returned to her hometown of Lawrence so that she could give birth to him with her parents nearby. Samuel and Jennie's children—first Leonard, followed by Shirley Anne in 1923 and Burton nine years after that—became the main thing that kept the couple together.

Jennie's mother insisted that the first child be named Louis after her father, even though both Samuel and Jennie preferred the name of Leonard. They always referred to their son by that name—or, more frequently, as Lenny—at home. That led to an embarrassing incident.

"When he [Leonard] first attended kindergarten, the teacher asked 'Louis Bernstein' to stand up," notes author Joan Peyser. "Recalling the incident, Bernstein said he had looked around the room for a boy with the same last name as his. But the teacher kept pointing at him. When he returned home and asked his mother about what had happened, she admitted his real name was Louis. From then until he turned sixteen, when he applied for his first driver's license and changed his name legally, all of Bernstein's report cards and official documents bore the name 'Louis.'"[2]

Confusion about names wasn't Leonard's only problem while he was growing up. From an early age, he was a sickly boy. He suffered from asthma and hay fever. In addition, the family moved several times. Because he was shy to start with, the shifts from apartment to apartment kept him from forming close friendships. He wasn't very good in sports, and other children often teased him. Sometimes the taunts were serious. Gangs of boys who were anti-Semitic frequently threatened Leonard.

Later in life he said, "You know what I lack talent in? Boxing. I can't hit anybody. It's one of the real shames of my life. I remember being attacked by a bully when I was just a kid, maybe because I was Jewish. I couldn't fight back."[3]

Leonard felt safest when he was home. His mother encouraged him and made him feel loved and supported.

Despite these problems, he always did well in school. He was also very imaginative. When they were 10, he and a friend named Eddie Ryack invented an imaginary country called Rybernia (from a combination of their last names). Rybernia had its own made-up language and social customs. Leonard allowed his sister and brother to become Rybernian citizens when they were old enough.

At about the time that Rybernia was established, Leonard came home one day and found a piano in his living room. His aunt was moving to New York. She offered the piano to the family. It was a momentous event in the shy boy's life.

"I was unhappy until I discovered music at the age of ten," he recalled. "Because I was a very sickly boy, I was small and pale, weak and always had some bronchitis or something. Suddenly I found my world; I became very strong inside and strangely enough around the same period I grew up very tall and I became athletic and was very strong, and I won medals and cups for diving. It all happened together and that changed my life. Because you see the secret of it is I found a universe where I was secure, where I was safe—that's music. Nobody could hurt me when I was in my world of music, sitting at that piano. There I was protected, I was at home."[4]

It also set up a conflict with his father. Samuel had begun his own business, the Samuel Bernstein Hair Company, at about the same time as Shirley's birth. He hoped that his children—especially Leonard, his eldest child—would follow in his footsteps and build up the company even more. That would give the family financial security. Samuel didn't approve of all the time his son was putting in on the piano. He was afraid it was taking time away from doing homework. Leonard's mother supported him, but his father was definitely the head of the household.

Yet when Leonard asked for a piano teacher, his father allowed him to hire one. Lenny soon became dissatisfied with his teacher and wanted another one, who was more expensive. His father refused. Money wasn't an issue. By then the country was in the first stages of the Great Depression. Unlike many other businesses during that time, the Samuel Bernstein Hair Company was doing very well.

Samuel's main concern was that his son might become so good that he would begin thinking of a career in music. He thought that musicians didn't make enough money. The only musicians with whom he was familiar were from his native Russia, known as *klezmorim*. They traveled from town to town, barely making enough money to survive. Memories of his days cleaning fish were still fresh in Samuel's mind. He didn't want Leonard to endure the same kind of poverty.

His father's objections didn't stop Leonard. The boy raised the extra money by giving lessons of his own and working part-time. His enthusiasm for music expanded. He organized neighborhood operas with his friends, did some improvising, and began composing.

Samuel finally gave grudging approval to the direction that Leonard's life was taking. He even went to a concert with Leonard when his son was 14. It was the first concert either of them had attended. Samuel also let Leonard perform on a radio program that his hair company sponsored.

Long after Leonard became famous, his father said, "Every genius had a handicap. Beethoven was deaf. Chopin had tuberculosis. Well, someday the books will say, 'Leonard Bernstein had a father.'"[5]

Leonard kept moving ahead. He asked Heinrich Gebhard, the region's best piano teacher, for lessons. Gebhard said Leonard wasn't quite ready, and referred him to Helen Coates, one of his assistants. Two years later, Leonard had improved enough to work directly with Gebhard.

Leonard graduated from the prestigious Boston Public Latin School in the spring of 1934 and entered Harvard University that fall. He continued to study music and took a number of other classes. One highlight was meeting noted American composer Aaron Copland in 1937. It was the beginning of a friendship that would last for many years.

With Leonard apparently headed toward a career as a pianist, 1937 also included another fateful meeting. A famous conductor named Dimitri Mitropoulos came to Boston to lead a performance of the Boston Symphony Orchestra. During his visit there was a tea party in his honor. Bernstein attended, and Mitropoulos asked him to play something on the piano. He was impressed enough to invite Bernstein to rehearsals. Sitting only a few feet away from the energetic and dynamic Mitropoulos, Bernstein fell under his spell. The idea of becoming a conductor entered his mind.

Two years later Bernstein made his debut as a conductor. He had composed the music for a student production of Greek playwright Aristophanes' *The Birds*.

Soon he graduated from Harvard—with excellent marks. His father allowed Bernstein to go to New York for the summer. He hoped that his son would realize that life in the big city was too risky financially. He would want to come home and take up a position with a guaranteed income with the Samuel Bernstein Hair Company.

Samuel appeared to be right. As Leonard recalled, "I finished the summer of '39 with no job and went home in defeat with $4 left in my pocket."[6]

A DEADLY EPIDEMIC

President Franklin
Delano Roosevelt

In March 1918, a few soldiers at a U.S. Army base in Kansas complained of illness. With the country in the midst of World War I, hardly anyone paid attention. Thousands of soldiers were sent to Europe to join in the fighting. They probably carried the germs with them. Some died in the closely packed trenches as an epidemic of influenza broke out.

Conditions became far worse in September when many of them began returning. An army hospital in Boston overflowed with sick men. Within weeks, the disease had spread to the civilian population. Soon the entire country felt its effects. President Woodrow Wilson and future president Franklin Delano Roosevelt both contracted the disease. They survived.

More than 675,000 of their countrymen did not. Nearly 200,000 died in October alone. It was not uncommon for people to wake up in the morning healthy and be dead by nightfall. In one case, three of four women who played cards one evening were dead within 24 hours. Mortuaries ran out of coffins. There were so many burials that funeral services had to be limited to 15 minutes. What was unusual was that the majority of the victims were between the ages of 20 and 40. Most epidemics target the very young or the very old. Yet this one attacked what was normally the healthiest segment of the population.

No part of the world was safe. Influenza ravaged people in every continent. Historians estimate between one fourth and one fifth of the earth's population became infected. More than 20 million people perished from it in less than a year. That made the disease much deadlier than World War I, in which between 10 and 15 million people died in four years. One reason for the extent of the crisis was that public health services were already burdened with wounded soldiers and civilians because of the effects of the war.

By the summer of 1919, the disease had run its course. It went away as mysteriously as it had arrived.

Leonard Bernstein studies a musical score as he prepares to lead an orchestral rehearsal early in his conducting career. Every conductor approaches a musical composition in a different manner. Sometimes conductors will become so familiar with a piece of music that they are able to conduct it entirely from memory.

CHAPTER
3

The Big Break

After leaving New York, Bernstein heard that Mitropoulos had recently returned to the United States from an overseas tour. Bernstein went to see him. Mitropoulos provided much-needed encouragement and arranged a special audition with Fritz Reiner, the conductor of the Pittsburgh Symphony Orchestra. Reiner was impressed and urged Bernstein to attend the Curtis Institute of Music in Philadelphia.

At first Bernstein didn't fit in. "Everybody at the Curtis Institute had come into the school eight years old, with short pants. I didn't have anybody to talk to. They hated me because they thought I was a snob, I was a Harvard graduate, an intellectual."[1]

Eventually the other students accepted him. Bernstein made good progress and in 1940 was invited to attend the famous Berkshire Music Festival (now known as the Tanglewood Music Festival) in western Massachusetts. There he met yet another important conductor, Serge Koussevitzky, who let Bernstein conduct the student orchestra. After Bernstein graduated from Curtis in 1941, Koussevitzky appointed him as his assistant the following summer.

Still, his career didn't seem to be advancing very rapidly. To make ends meet, Bernstein took a job with a music publishing company. In his spare time, he composed some music.

Although the Berkshire Music Festival was canceled in 1943 because of World War II, Koussevitzky was still there. He wanted Bernstein to conduct a special fund-raising concert. On August 25, Bernstein received an unexpected birthday present. He met Artur Rodzinski, the new conductor of the New York Philharmonic, one of the country's oldest and most prestigious orchestras. Rodzinski had heard Bernstein conduct at Tanglewood. Now he had a startling offer. He offered Bernstein the post of assistant conductor of the New York Philharmonic.

The only downside was that assistant conductors almost never have the chance to lead the orchestra in public concerts. Rodzinski and established guest conductors always served in that role. While Bernstein's father was pleased that the job came with a good salary, he made it clear that his son could still come to work with him.

It was the last time he would make the offer. Leonard Bernstein was about to be catapulted into fame.

The famous Bruno Walter was scheduled to conduct the New York Philharmonic on Sunday afternoon, November 14, 1943. Bernstein had been up late the night before attending a party. The telephone woke him from a sound slumber. Bernstein heard the astonishing news that Walter was too sick to get out of bed. Rodzinski was out of town and couldn't return in time to replace him. Bernstein would have to conduct the orchestra.

There was no time for a rehearsal. It was pressure enough to be in front of several thousand concertgoers in Carnegie Hall, where the performance would take place. But those people would be only a small portion of the audience. The performance was also being broadcast live on radio all across the nation.

Bernstein had some preparation. He'd attended all of Walter's rehearsals with the orchestra. He was familiar with the music. On his way to Carnegie Hall, he stopped by Walter's hotel room and spoke briefly with the ailing conductor.

The concert got off to a shaky start. The orchestra manager came on stage to announce that Bruno Walter was ill and wouldn't appear. Some people in the audience muttered their

Bruno Walter was born in 1876 in Berlin, Germany. A child prodigy as a pianist, he became a conductor at the age of 17 and soon became internationally famous. He conducted every major orchestra and made scores of recordings, remaining active well into his 80s. He died in 1962.

disappointment to their neighbors. A few even got up and went home. As Bernstein walked to the podium, he was greeted by some scattered, polite applause.

Two hours later, the reaction was entirely different. Bernstein's brother Burton remembered, "When the concert ended, the house roared like some giant animal in a zoo. It was certainly the loudest human sound I have ever heard—thrilling and eerie."[2]

The orchestra joined in the ovation. One member said, "The idea was, he'd follow us, only it didn't work out that way. You just couldn't believe a young man could create that kind of music. Here were players in their fifties and sixties with long experience. And here this little snot-nose comes in and creates a more exciting performance. We were supposed to have gone over it with Bruno Walter, we had rehearsed it with him and performed it with him, and this had nothing to do with Bruno Walter. The orchestra stood up and cheered. We were open-mouthed. That man was the most extraordinary musician I have met in my life."[3]

The *New York Times* joined in the chorus of approval. "Mr. Bernstein had to have something approaching genius to make full use of his opportunity," the paper said in an editorial. "It's a good American success story. The warm, friendly triumph of it filled Carnegie Hall and spread far over the air waves."[4]

Leonard Bernstein was an overnight sensation. But he was hardly a flash in the pan. He would remain at the forefront of the American musical scene for nearly half a century. ◆

THE NATION OF ISRAEL IS ESTABLISHED

Palestine

Not long after the birth of Jesus, Jews were expelled from their homes in what is today Palestine and forced to move somewhere else. In many of the places they settled, they were frequently persecuted. Starting in the 1880s, some Jewish leaders began to advocate reestablishing a homeland in Palestine. Jewish immigration to the area slowly began to increase.

During World War I, the Turkish Ottoman Empire—of which Palestine was a part—supported Germany. When the war ended, the victorious British took over the responsibility for administering Palestine. They soon became caught in the middle of an escalating conflict. Their Balfour Declaration of 1917 seemed to promise the Jews an independent state in Palestine. Yet the British also tried to please the Arab population, which was becoming increasingly angry as more and more Jews arrived.

Tensions heightened after World War II. For many people, the horrors of the Holocaust seemed to demonstrate the need for a Jewish state. Even more Jews wanted to get into Palestine, but the British tried to keep them out. It became harder for them to maintain order. Finally they turned the situation over to the United Nations. In 1947, the United Nations General Assembly voted to partition Palestine, creating separate Jewish and Arab states. The Jews welcomed the news. Arabs were outraged.

As soon as independence became official on May 14, 1948, armies from five neighboring countries attacked. After several months of fighting, the Israelis were victorious. During the conflict, hundreds of thousands of Arabs were displaced from Palestine. A similar number of Jews were forced to leave Arab countries. Many of those Jews moved to Israel to establish new homes. The majority of the Arabs went into refugee camps that have endured for decades.

Since then, the region has remained one of the world's most troubled areas. Several efforts at establishing a lasting peace have broken down due to mutual distrust and hatred.

Leonard Bernstein prepares to lead a concert in 1954, when he was 36 and had been famous for a decade. By this time he had also become well-established as a composer.

CHAPTER

4

Success After Success

Bernstein's triumph as a conductor was followed by the premieres of two of his compositions. His Symphony No. 1, also known as "Jeremiah," drew on his Jewish heritage; it was his first major composition. It premiered in January 1944 and won the New York Music Critics Award.

Three months later, he conducted the premiere of a ballet score he had written in collaboration with choreographer Jerome Robbins. Called *Fancy Free,* it was yet another example of the good luck that seemed to follow Bernstein around. Robbins had had an idea for the adventures of three sailors on shore leave. He approached a composer, but he didn't like the music that the man gave him. During a walk in New York's Central Park, Robbins met a friend who suggested Bernstein. Since Central Park was very close to Carnegie Hall, they dropped in on him. After discussing the ballet for a few minutes, Bernstein improvised some themes on the piano. That was all it took. Robbins quickly agreed that Bernstein was the man he wanted.

Fancy Free was a big hit. It played 200 times during its first year, and every time it was a sellout.

Even ill health turned out well for Bernstein that year. He had to go into the hospital for an operation. By chance, a well-known librettist named Adolph Green was also there. Bernstein made sure that they had rooms next to each other. That way they would have the chance for long talks. By the time they were discharged, Bernstein and Green—along with Green's songwriting partner, Betty Comden—had agreed to collaborate on making *Fancy Free* into a full-fledged Broadway musical.

This photo shows a production of the ballet Fancy Free in London, England's Covent Garden in 1946, two years after its premiere. Leonard Bernstein wrote the music. It was choreographed by Jerome Robbins, who also performed in this production. He is the sailor on the left.

Known as *On the Town,* it was an immediate sensation when it made its debut at the end of 1944.

Virtually unknown just 13 months before, Leonard Bernstein was now one of the most famous figures in American music. Offers flooded in. So did letters, requests for interviews, and everything else that comes with fame. One of his first tasks was to hire a secretary. Interestingly, his choice was his former piano teacher, Helen Coates. It was a successful choice, as she remained in that position for many years.

Despite everything, Bernstein remained humble. "I couldn't believe that all this was happening to me. I didn't really believe it was me at all. Me—a celebrity!"[1]

To take advantage of all the offers, he resigned as assistant conductor of the New York Philharmonic. He soon was offered the job as chief conductor for the newly formed New York City Symphony, a post he held for three years. He liked the opportunity of planning the music for an orchestra. Meanwhile, he could still take on a number of guest conducting assignments.

When World War II ended in 1945, Bernstein was able to travel to Europe and conduct concerts there. In 1947, a year before the Jewish state of Israel came into existence, he visited the Jewish sector of Palestine. It was a moving experience for him to visit the spiritual home of the Jewish religion. He returned the following year, shortly after Israel became independent. Israel was in the midst of a bloody war with several nearby Arab countries that were trying to destroy it. Despite personal danger, Bernstein remained for three months as director of the Israel Philharmonic Orchestra. He conducted a number of open-air concerts with Israeli troops standing guard. He enjoyed a close relationship with the orchestra for the rest of his life.

In 1951 he married Felicia Montealegre, a Chilean actress whom he had met five years earlier. They would have three children: Jamie Anne Marie, born in 1952; Alexander Serge Leonard, born in 1955 (his second name honored Serge Koussevitzky); and Nina Maria Felicia, born in 1962.

Soon Bernstein expanded the range of his interests. He wrote the musical score for the 1954 dramatic film *On the Waterfront*. The film won eight Academy Awards the following year, including Best Picture. Its star, Marlon Brando, won an Oscar for Best Actor. While Bernstein received a nomination, he didn't win.

He didn't let that bother him. He was already moving on to new projects. At that time, television was still a relative newcomer to the American entertainment scene. TV sets were large, often cumbersome, and the pictures were in black and white. Yet Bernstein saw that it had great potential for communicating his passion for music to much larger audiences than could attend live performances.

His first television program was called *Omnibus*. It was intended for adults. Rather than giving a stuffy lecture, Bernstein provided visual effects. For example, he had the entire floor of the set painted with the notes from the first page of Ludwig van Beethoven's Fifth Symphony. As his musicians played the music, Bernstein walked from note to note. He wanted to show how the entire first movement of the symphony came from its four dramatic opening notes: *duh-duh-duh-duuuhhh*.

He was about to write his own dramatic work. It would make him even more famous. ◆

MARLON BRANDO

Marlon Brando

Marlon Brando is perhaps best known among today's moviegoers for his portrayal of Don Vito Corleone in *The Godfather* trilogy. He was born in Omaha, Nebraska, in 1924 to Dorothy and Marlon Brando. His mother was involved in local theaters. Marlon probably picked up his interest in acting from her. He had a difficult childhood and was expelled from several schools. Once he rode a motorcycle in the halls.

In 1943 Brando moved to New York City to attend acting school. A year later, he appeared on Broadway in the play *I Remember Mama*.

His first major hit came in 1947 when he portrayed Stanley Kowalski in the play *A Streetcar Named Desire*. He also starred in the movie version of *Streetcar* in 1951, receiving an Academy Award nomination for his work. He expressed his rebellious side and made one of Hollywood's most memorable movie posters by playing a leather-jacketed biker in *The Wild One. On the Waterfront* (Bernstein wrote the musical score) established him as a major star. Though he appeared in a number of films after that—such as *Guys and Dolls, The Teahouse of the August Moon, The Young Lions,* and *Mutiny on the Bounty*—his career went into a long decline starting in the early 1960s.

The Godfather, which was released in 1972, restored his major star status and earned him another Oscar for Best Actor. After that, he made films such as *Superman, Apocalypse Now, Don Juan DeMarco* (this 1995 film featured Johnny Depp in one of the first major roles of his career), and *The Score*.

Because Brando was very influential among his fellow actors, tributes poured in when he died in July 2004. He was especially famous for "method acting," in which an actor taps into his or her emotions to create a character. *Time* magazine, which put him on its cover several times, called him one of the 100 most important people of the 20th century.

This scene from the movie version of *West Side Story* shows several members of the Jets, one of the two teenage gangs whose conflict drives the film's action, in a lively dance on the streets of New York. Russ Tamblyn, wearing the yellow jacket, plays the role of Riff, the gang's leader.

CHAPTER 5

West Side Story

Early in 1949, Jerome Robbins called Bernstein with an idea. He wanted to do an updated musical version of William Shakespeare's tragedy *Romeo and Juliet.*

In *Romeo and Juliet,* the conflict is between two families, the Montagues and the Capulets, who detest each other with a passion that sometimes turns deadly. Each family has just one child: Romeo Montague and Juliet Capulet. As teenagers, they see each other at a dance and instantly fall in love. Because of the hatred their families feel for each other, they can meet only in secret. They make plans to run away. But those plans fall apart and the young lovers both die.

Under Robbins' idea, the conflict would be between Jews and Irish Catholics rather than two families. For Bernstein and for Robbins, that conflict was all too real.

"Bernstein was raised in a predominantly Jewish suburb of Boston that bordered an area populated by working-class Irish Catholics," writes Mary Williams. "On occasion, when he wandered too far from his neighborhood, Catholic youths would physically attack him for being 'short and Jewish.'"[1]

Conditions were also grim for Robbins, who "experienced the same social anti-Semitism; he was also ridiculed for being a male who relished the violin, painting, and dance. His father vehemently opposed his youthful dreams of becoming a ballet dancer. As Robbins' sister Sonia recalls, their father would yell at Jerome, 'You should be a shoemaker! You don't have a boy dancing in a Jewish family.'"[2]

The two men soon agreed on a name: *East Side Story,* after the actual Manhattan neighborhood where their story would take place. They also agreed that Arthur Laurents would write the libretto. The three men set to work, but they were all so busy and so frequently on the road that it was hard to spend enough time on the project. There was another concern. Religious conflicts had been around for so long that they had lost their sense of immediacy. The men were afraid that their idea might not seem very relevant.

"We had another meeting in New York and decided to give it up," Bernstein wrote. "We didn't bury it, but we decided to sleep on it."[3]

It turned out to be a long rest. More than five years later, Laurents and Bernstein were sitting by the pool at a hotel in Los Angeles. "We were saying what a shame it was the show never came to fruition," Bernstein recalled. "We looked at a Los Angeles newspaper somebody had left on a chair and noticed this huge headline, 'Gang riots on Olvera Street.' Fights had broken out between Mexicans and so-called Americans. A light bulb went off. Why didn't we think of that in the first place? The East Side wasn't where it was happening."[4]

That was all it took. Bernstein continued, "We're fired again by the Romeo notion; only now we have abandoned the whole Jewish-Catholic premise as not very fresh, and have come up with what I think is going to be it: two teen-age gangs, one the warring Puerto Ricans, the other self-styled 'Americans.' Suddenly it all springs to life. I hear rhythms and pulses, and—most of all—I can sort of feel the form."[5]

Because Bernstein was committed to working on another musical, *Candide,* the Romeo story once again had to take a nap. But early in 1957 he was finally able to work on it without interruption. By then the original three-man creative team had added a fourth member: a young songwriter named Stephen Sondheim. The action had shifted to the other side of Manhattan, and the play became known as *West Side Story.*

The opposing factions reflect 1950s social divisions. One of the gangs, the Sharks, consists of young Puerto Ricans who have recently come to the United States. The other gang is the Jets. They are "Americans," the sons of European immigrants who arrived in this country one or two generations before. The members of each gang and their female admirers don't see their opponents as people, only as stereotypes. That makes it easier for them to blindly hate each other.

Romeo is Tony, the best friend of Riff, the leader of the Jets. Juliet is Maria. She is the sister of Bernardo, the leader of the Sharks. She is engaged to Bernardo's friend Chino, but doesn't seem to care for him very much.

Tony and Maria meet at a dance and immediately fall in love. Afterward, in a version of the famous balcony scene in *Romeo and Juliet,* they swear their love for each other. They meet again the following evening and even go through a pretend marriage ceremony.

But just as Shakespeare's young lovers are not destined for happiness, so too are Tony and Maria starting out on a doomed love. The blind hatred the two gangs feel for each other leads to tragedy and death.

There was nothing tragic about the reception given to *West Side Story*. It ran for two years on Broadway, went on the road, and then returned to Broadway for another series of sellout performances. While the stage version did very well, the show's real popularity came in 1961 when it made its film debut. Starring Natalie Wood as Maria and Richard Beymer as Tony, *West Side Story* became a huge hit. It ranked second in box office receipts to *101 Dalmatians*. At the Academy Awards the following year, *West Side Story* won 10 Oscars, including the coveted Best Picture. Other Oscars included Robert Wise and Jerome Robbins (Best Director), George Chakiris (Best Supporting Actor, as Bernardo) and Rita Moreno (Best Supporting Actress, as Anita). Bernstein almost certainly would have won an Oscar as well, but his score wasn't eligible because it was no longer original.

There wasn't any doubt about the realism of the various sites in New York City where the filming took place. One time the actors and crew were pelted with rocks from a nearby building. In another location, police protection wasn't good enough. The producers had to hire a street gang to keep the actors safe.

Because of the movie, *West Side Story* is probably Bernstein's most famous composition. The sound track and home video versions remain top sellers even today. Countless numbers of viewers still enjoy Bernstein's music, which ranges from classical to lively Latin American rhythms. ◆

ROMEO AND JULIET ON THE SILVER SCREEN

Romeo and Juliet

Though *Romeo and Juliet* was written more than 400 years ago, its themes of young love and the tragic consequences of blind hatred make it one of William Shakespeare's most popular plays. Many professional and amateur theaters perform it every year.

It has also been made into dozens of movies. Three of these versions continue to do well as home video rentals or sales.

The first was Italian director Franco Zeffirelli's 1968 production. Previous film versions featured adults as the teenaged lovers. Zeffirelli broke with that tradition by casting 17-year-old Leonard Whiting as Romeo and 15-year-old Olivia Hussey as Juliet. Their youth not only makes them totally believable in their parts, but also creates instant identification among their fellow teenagers in the audience. Zeffirelli used a number of Italian locations that had changed very little during the course of several centuries to give the same period feel of previous movies. His *Romeo and Juliet* was nominated for four Academy Awards and won two Oscars.

In 1996, the play underwent a major update with Leonardo DiCaprio and Claire Danes as the stars. Director Baz Luhrmann (who later directed *Moulin Rouge!*, starring Nicole Kidman) switched the location from Verona, Italy, to Verona Beach, Florida. The time is the present. Everyone wears modern-day dress. Pistols replace swords. Cars replace horses. Constantly changing camera angles suggest the style of a rock video.

Four years later, *Romeo Must Die* loosely adapted the play. The scene shifts to Oakland, California. The primary conflict is between Asian and African-American gangs. The movie stars Chinese martial arts actor Jet Li, who created a sensation in the United States in 1998's *Lethal Weapon 4*. "Romeo" (renamed Han Sing) falls in love with "Juliet" (now called Trish O'Day, a role played by Aaliyah), the daughter of the head of the rival gang. But their romance is less important than the almost constant martial arts fight sequences.

This photo of Leonard Bernstein was taken during the early 1970s, not long after his retirement as music director of the New York Philharmonic. He remained very active as a composer, guest conductor and lecturer until the end of his life, communicating the joy that he felt about music to countless numbers of people.

CHAPTER 6

An All-Encompassing Career

The premiere of *West Side Story* was followed early in 1958 by Bernstein's appointment as music director of the New York Philharmonic. That honor put him in a unique situation. He was the only man to achieve overwhelming success in both theatrical and classical music at the same time.

A few weeks later, he performed his first annual Young People's Concert. These concerts weren't new. The scope of the audience was. In addition to packed houses of youngsters and their parents at Carnegie Hall, Bernstein arranged for the programs to be televised. They were broadcast during the next 15 years, and many are still available on video recordings. Young viewers enjoyed Bernstein's ability to make music interesting. To appeal to them, Bernstein often used pop stars such as the Beatles or Jimi Hendrix for his music examples. He genuinely loved all types of music and wanted to convey that passion.

The success of his television programs soon led Bernstein in yet another direction. He became an author. His first book, *The Joy of Music,* was published in 1959. Several more—including *Leonard Bernstein's Young People's Concerts*—would follow.

Bernstein put most of his energy during the 1960s into the New York Philharmonic. Soon after retiring in 1969, he was saddened by the death of his father. Samuel had long since realized how gifted Leonard was and became very proud of his son. By then, Bernstein had become controversial. He opposed the Vietnam War. He was also very involved in the Civil Rights movement. He briefly separated from his wife in the mid-1970s. They were soon reconciled, but Felicia died shortly afterward of lung cancer.

Despite these difficulties, Bernstein continued with his hectic schedule. His energy and enthusiasm remained at their usual high levels. But another difficulty was harder to deal with. It was ill health. In 1986, he said, "I was diagnosed as having emphysema in my mid-20s and I've been smoking for decades. I was told that if I didn't stop, I'd be dead by age 35. Then they said I'd be dead by age 45. And 55. Well, I beat the rap. I smoke, I drink, I stay up all night. . . . I'm overcommitted on all fronts."[1]

Bernstein couldn't cheat death forever. He often told people that he wanted to die while he was conducting. He may have been thinking of Dimitri Mitropoulos, who suffered a fatal heart attack in 1960 while leading a rehearsal. Soon after his triumphant appearance in Berlin, Bernstein received some awful news. During an examination to discover the cause of ongoing back pain, physicians found something else. He had a malignant tumor on his left lung. Despite the pain and discomfort of radiation treatments, Bernstein kept going, but on a lighter schedule.

There was one date on his schedule that he knew he had to keep. The 50th anniversary celebration of the Tanglewood Music Festival was slated for August 19, 1990. Dedicated to the memory of Serge Koussevitzky, it would be held in the concert hall that Koussevitzky established, and played by the orchestra that

Koussevitzky founded. Bernstein still felt a deep debt of gratitude to Koussevitzky.

The program consisted of three works. The second one was Bernstein's own *Arias and Barcarolles,* the final work he composed. He was so exhausted that an assistant had to conduct it. Then in the midst of Beethoven's Seventh Symphony—part of his first program as conductor of the New York Philharmonic more than 30 years earlier— Bernstein suddenly stopped, pulled out a handkerchief, and suffered a long fit of coughing. For the rest of the performance he could barely nod his head in time to the music.

Seven weeks later, he was dead. Bernstein suffered a heart attack at home on the evening of October 14, 1990, and died almost instantly. Even though he was 72, some people thought that he was too young to die, since he always radiated so much energy. Half-jokingly, composer Ned Rorem said, "Lenny led four lives in one, so he was not 72 but 288."[2] Rorem was referring to Bernstein's major contributions as a composer, conductor, pianist, and teacher. His achievements in any one of these areas would have constituted a satisfying career. To reach such high levels in all four was something that no other American had ever done.

The title of his book *The Joy of Music* summed up his life. He believed that music made life much richer. His energy and his love for music influenced countless numbers of people.

"Hailed as a hero, Bernstein was able to popularize the classics in a way that no previous musician had ever done," writes music critic Peter Gutmann. "An entire generation of Americans was drawn to great music through his television shows. Anyone who attended a Bernstein concert left feeling the profound wonder not only of music but of life itself. No musician in the history of America touched so many people so deeply and in so many ways."[3]

Selected Works

Music for Theater and Film
Fancy Free
On the Town
Trouble in Tahiti
Wonderful Town
On the Waterfront
Candide
West Side Story
Dybbuk
A Quiet Place

Orchestral Works
Symphony No. 1 ("Jeremiah")
Symphony No. 2 ("The Age of Anxiety")

Symphony No. 3 ("Kaddish")
Prelude, Fugue and Riffs
Serenade
Concerto for Orchestra

Vocal Works
Chichester Psalms
Mass
*Songfest: A Cycle of American Poems for
Six Singers and Orchestra*
Missa Brevis
Arias and Barcarolles

Chronology

1918	Born on August 25 in Lawrence, Massachusetts
1928	Receives piano from aunt and begins taking lessons
1929	Enters Boston Public Latin School
1934	Performs first piano recital; enters Harvard University
1939	Makes first appearance as conductor; graduates, with honors, from Harvard
1940	First appearance as conductor with professional orchestra
1943	Stands in as conductor for ailing Bruno Walter to great acclaim
1944	Symphony No. 1 ("Jeremiah"), *Fancy Free,* and *On the Town* premiere
1947	Conducts concerts in Palestine
1951	Marries actress Felicia Montealegre
1952	Birth of daughter Jamie
1955	Birth of son, Alexander Serge Leonard

1957	*West Side Story* premieres
1958	Appointed as music director of New York Philharmonic; begins annually televising Young People's Concerts
1959	Publishes *The Joy of Music*
1961	Film version of *West Side Story* opens
1962	Birth of daughter Nina
1964	Makes conducting debut
1969	Father dies; leads his last concert of New York Philharmonic as music director
1971	Inaugurates John F. Kennedy Center for the Performing Arts in Washington, D.C., with his *Mass*
1973	Leads Concert for Peace in Washington, D.C., to oppose President Nixon on the eve of Nixon's second term in office
1977	Conducts two of his songs at Inaugural Concert for President Jimmy Carter
1978	Wife, Felicia, dies
1980	Receives Kennedy Center Honor for Lifetime of Contributions to American Culture through the Performing Arts
1989	Conducts Berlin Freedom Concerts to celebrate the reunification of Germany
1990	Dies on October 14 in New York City
1993	The corner of Broadway and 65th Street in New York City is renamed Leonard Bernstein Place; Tanglewood Music Center opens its Leonard Bernstein Campus
1999	Public Broadcasting System releases *Leonard Bernstein: Reaching for the Note,* a film about Bernstein's life and career
2003	DVD Special Edition of *West Side Story* is released
2004	Production of *West Side Story* begins five-month, six-city German tour

1842	Several prominent musicians found the New York Philharmonic Society, which eventually becomes known as the New York Philharmonic.
1868	President Andrew Johnson is impeached, but the U.S. Senate acquits him by a single vote.
1879	Gilbert and Sullivan operetta *H.M.S. Pinafore* creates a sensation when it appears in the United States.
1882	Russian composer Igor Stravinsky is born.
1888	American songwriter Irving Berlin is born.
1901	Jazz trumpeter Louis Armstrong is born.
1913	New York City's Grand Central Terminal opens.
1918	World War II ends after more than four years of fighting and more than 10 million deaths.
1920	The Eighteenth Amendment goes into effect; known as Prohibition, it forbids the sale and manufacture of alcoholic beverages in the United States.
1923	Henry Luce and Briton Hadden launch *Time* magazine.
1927	U.S. pilot Charles Lindbergh becomes the first person to make a solo flight across the Atlantic Ocean.
1929	The U.S. stock market crash brings about the Great Depression.
1933	The Eighteenth Amendment is repealed.
1936	King Edward VIII of Great Britain gives up his throne to marry American divorcée Wallis Simpson.
1941	New York Yankee outfielder Joe DiMaggio has a base hit in 56 straight games to set a Major League Baseball record.
1946	Aurele "Al" Couture knocks out Ralph Walton is less than 11 seconds, the shortest-ever recorded boxing match.
1949	"Rudolph the Red-Nosed Reindeer" makes its debut and becomes one of the year's most popular songs.
1954	USS *Nautilus* becomes the world's first nuclear-powered submarine.
1959	*The Sound of Music* premieres on Broadway.
1963	President John F. Kennedy is assassinated.
1968	Richard M. Nixon is elected as U.S. President.
1971	Louis Armstrong dies.
1974	President Nixon resigns rather than face impeachment charges.
1978	Supertanker *Amoco Cadiz* breaks up off the Normandy coast of France, blackening more than 100 miles of coastline with oil.
1989	Irving Berlin dies.
1990	American composer Aaron Copland dies.
1991	U.S.-led coalition defeats Iraq in the first Gulf War but leaves Saddam Hussein in power.
1999	Louis Sachar's book *Holes* wins the Newbery Medal as the best children's book.
2004	*Lord of the Rings: Return of the King* wins 13 Oscars to tie the all-time record.

Chapter Notes

Chapter 1   The Wall Comes Tumbling Down

1. CNN Cold War—"Episode 9: The Wall," http://www.cnn.com/SPECIALS/cold.war/episodes/09/1st.draft/.

2. Meryle Secrest, *Leonard Bernstein: A Life* (New York: Alfred A. Knopf, 1994), p. 401.

Chapter 2   The Discovery of Music

1. Paul Myers, *Leonard Bernstein* (London: Phaidon Press Limited, 1998), p. 14.

2. Joan Peyser, *Bernstein: A Biography* (New York: Billboard Books, 1998), p. 21.

3. Meryle Secrest, *Leonard Bernstein: A Life* (New York: Alfred A. Knopf, 1994), p. 14.

4. Peter Gradenwitz, *Leonard Bernstein: The Infinite Variety of a Musician* (New York: Oswald Woolf Books, 1987), p. 22.

5. Classical Notes—"Leonard Bernstein: A Total Embrace of Music," http://www.classicalnotes.net/features/bernstein.html.

6. Secrest, p. 59.

Chapter 3   The Big Break

1. Peter Gradenwitz, *Leonard Bernstein: The Infinite Variety of a Musician* (New York: Oswald Woolf Books, 1987), p. 29.

2. Ibid., p. 35.

3. Meryle Secrest, *Leonard Bernstein: A Life* (New York: Alfred A. Knopf, 1994), p. 118.

4. Gradenwitz, p. 37.

Chapter 4   Success After Success

1. Peter Gradenwitz, *Leonard Bernstein: The Infinite Variety of a Musician* (New York: Oswald Woolf Books, 1987), p. 40.

Chapter 5   West Side Story

1. Mary E. Williams, editor, *Readings on West Side Story* (San Diego, Calif.: Greenhaven Press, 2001), p. 15.

2. Ibid., p. 16.

3. Ibid., p. 39.

4. Ibid.

5. Ibid., p. 44.

Chapter 6   An All-Encompassing Career

1. Joan Peyser, *Bernstein: A Biography* (New York: Billboard Books, 1998), p. 16.

2. Classical Notes—"Leonard Bernstein: A Total Embrace of Music," http://www.classicalnotes.net/features/bernstein.html.Classical Notes.

3. Ibid.

Glossary

anti-Semitic (AN-tye seh-MIH-tic)—having prejudice against or hostility toward Jewish people or their religion and culture.

ballet (bal-LAY)—theatrical presentation in which the story is told through dancing with musical accompaniment.

choreographer (core-ee-AH-gruh-fer)—a person who makes up the steps in a ballet or other dance.

libretto (lih-BREH-toe)—the words to an opera or other musical performance.

opera (AH-p'rah)—a drama set to music, with all or most of the dialogue sung.

Oscar (OS-ker)—an award given by the Academy of Motion Picture Arts and Sciences for excellence in the movie industry; it is also called an Academy Award.

premiere (preh-MEER)—the first performance of a new artistic work.

rabbi (RAB-bye)—the leader of a Jewish congregation.

symphony (SIM-foe-nee)—a large-scale musical composition for full orchestra, usually consisting of four parts, or movements.

Talmud (TAHL-mud)—commentaries and interpretations of the Torah, compiled in two documents: the Mishnah and the Gemara.

Torah (TORE-uh)—the five books of Moses in the Bible (Genesis, Exodus, Leviticus, Numbers, Deuteronomy), which hold the basic laws and teachings of the Jewish religion.

For Further Reading

For Young Adults

Bernstein, Leonard. *Young People's Concerts*. New York: Anchor, 1992.

Blashfield, Jean. *Leonard Bernstein: Composer and Conductor*. New York: Ferguson Publishing, 2000.

Hurwitz, Johanna. *Leonard Bernstein: A Passion for Music*. Philadelphia: Jewish Publication Society, 1993.

Lazo, Caroline Evenson. *Leonard Bernstein: In Love With Music*. Minneapolis: Lerner Publications, 2002.

Williams, Mary E. (editor). *Readings on West Side Story*. San Diego, Calif.: Greenhaven Press, 2001.

Works Consulted

Gradenwitz, Peter. *Leonard Bernstein: The Infinite Variety of a Musician*. New York: Oswald Woolf Books, 1987.

Myers, Paul. *Leonard Bernstein*. London: Phaidon Press Limited, 1998.

Peyser, Joan. *Bernstein: A Biography*. New York: Billboard Books, 1998.

Secrest, Meryle. *Leonard Bernstein: A Life*. New York: Alfred A. Knopf, 1994.

Seiler, Thomas. *Leonard Bernstein: The Last Ten Years*. New York: Stemmle Publishers, 1999.

On the Internet

The Official Leonard Bernstein Web Site
http://www.leonardbernstein.com

Sony Classical—"Leonard Bernstein"
http://www.sonyclassical.com/artists/
bernstein/

Arias and Barcarolles—The Leonard Bernstein Pages
http://www.users.globalnet.co.uk/
-mcgoni/

American Masters—"Leonard Bernstein"
http://www.pbs.org/wnet/
americanmasters/database/
bernstein_l.html

Classical Notes—"Leonard Bernstein: A Total Embrace of Music"
http://www.classicalnotes.net/features/
bernstein.html

Turner Classic Movies—West Side Story
http://www.turnerclassicmovies.com/
ThisMonth/Article/
0,,66963|66964|21744,00.html

CNN Cold War—"Episode 9: The Wall"
http://www.cnn.com/SPECIALS/
cold.war/episodes/09/1st.draft/

Cuban Missile Crisis
"The Cuban Missile Crisis"
http://www.hpol.org/jfk/cuban/

A Deadly Epidemic
The American Experience—"Influenza 1918"
http://www.pbs.org/wgbh/amex/
influenza/

Index